Copyright © 2021 by Me Myself & Family

All rights reserved. No part of this publication may be reproduced, distributed, or transmitted in any form or by any means, including photo-copying, recording, or other electronic or mechanical methods, without the prior written permission of the publisher, except in the case of brief quotations embodied in critical reviews and certain other noncommercial uses permitted by copyright law. For permission requests, write to the author, addressed "Attention: Permissions" at barteap@me-myself-family.com.

# Introduction

Can you think of a time where you needed more peace in your life?

I know I can. And because I am human, I still have moments that compromise my peace- **but not as often**. And why is that? Well simply put, I learned how to practice mindfulness, through **positive affirmations!**

In this book, I give you 15 of the most powerful affirmations and how to use them for meditation, reflection, and journaling. Whether the affirmation is about energy, nature, or forgiveness- each affirmation has allowed me to create more positivity, peace, and balance in my life. I know they will do the same for you.

Sidenote- to take your affirmation journey to another level, [check out my positive affirmation journal and calendar](). Both will give you the opportunity to write down your thoughts and feelings per affirmation. Absolutely amazing!

# TABLE OF CONTENTS

### 03
I will trust my inner jouney.

### 05
I put energy into that matter to me.

### 07
I give myself the care and attention that I deserve.

### 09
I forgive myself for not being perfect, because I am human.

### 11
I show gratitude to those who love me.

### 13
I live a peaceful life.

### 15
I create and maintain healthy boundaries.

### 17
I learn something new everyday.

### 19
I enjoy and appreciate nature.

### 21
I share my experiences, to help others.

### 23
I have the power to crush my goals.

### 25
I release negative people or energy from my life.

### 27
My smile brightens every space that I am in.

### 29
I use wisdom to make the best decisions.

### 31
I am honest with myself and others.

*Affirmation 01.*

**I WILL TRUST MY INNER JOURNEY.**

## 01.  I will trust my inner journey.

An inner journey is an **unfolding** process of personal thoughts and emotions.

An inner journey can be full of positivity, but also unwelcomed situations and circumstances.

Just remember: regardless of how you feel, the journey is needed for personal growth. It's **your** personal journey. No one can live it for you. Just know that it will manifest into greatness over your life.

**_Reflection:_** *Think about your inner journey. What type of emotions do you feel? What do you want to achieve by the end of the journey? Who are you becoming?*

*Affirmation 02.*

---

**I PUT ENERGY INTO
THINGS THAT MATTER TO ME.**

---

## 02. I put energy into things that matter to me.

When you put energy into things that matter to you, you dictate what comes into your life, and what should be removed.

Focusing on the things that matter also allows you to manifest greatness for someone else, or over a specific project.

And don't forget that this is also a form of self-care because you are spending time on things or people that are assets to your mental health.

**_Reflection:_** *What matters to you? Is it family, friends, career, your business? Make a list. Write down how you could spend more time on the things from the list. Put the effort in. You will begin to slowly remove things that waste your time, while adding things that you value.*

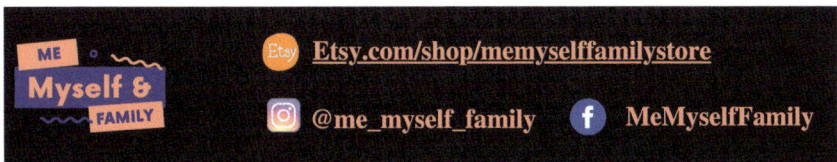

*Affirmation 03.*

---

## I GIVE MYSELF THE CARE AND ATTENTION THAT I DESERVE.

---

## 03. I give myself the care and attention that I deserve.

Self-care can be tangible or intangible. For example, buying an outfit (tangible) and spending time meditating (intangible) are both forms of self-care.

Giving yourself care and attention is important because it allows you to refresh and renew the body and spirit. Recharging is necessary!

You have to love and care for yourself before you can truly care for anyone else.

**_Reflection:_** *What makes you feel good or peaceful? Make a list. Pick items from the list and add them to your routine. Tip: Start with self-care Sundays. Every Sunday, pick two items off of your list and dedicate time without any interruptions.*

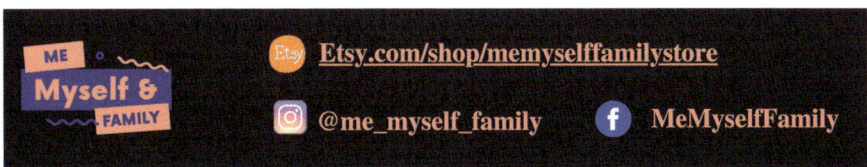

*Affirmation 04.*

---

## I FORGIVE MYSELF FOR NOT BEING PERFECT, BECAUSE I AM HUMAN.

---

## 04. I forgive myself for not being perfect, because I am human.

When you forgive yourself for past decisions, you begin to embrace your imperfections.

Forgiving yourself clears your mind so that you can have more positive thoughts.

Self forgiveness is also a form of self-care. Give yourself some grace!

**_Reflection:_** *What do you blame yourself for? What do you wish you would have done differently? What was the lesson learned? How will you handle similar situations in the future? Forgive yourself, and focus on the lesson. This is how you thrive.*

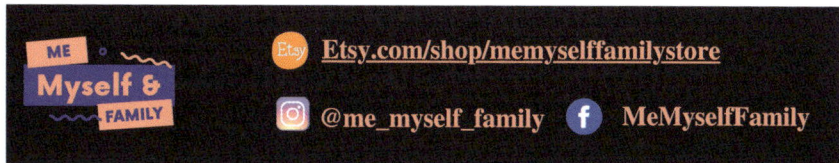

*Affirmation 05.*

**I SHOW GRATITUDE TO THOSE WHO LOVE ME.**

## 05.    I show gratitude to those who love me.

Gratitude shows your loved ones how thankful you are, and it also provides self-contentment.

It unshackles you from toxic emotions.

Studies over the past decade show that people who consciously show appreciation for others tend to be happier and less depressed. It's good for your mental health.

**_Reflection:_** Who are you grateful for? What do you appreciate about them? Keep in mind that gratitude is valuable to your mental health, even if you can't share it with the person that you're thankful for.

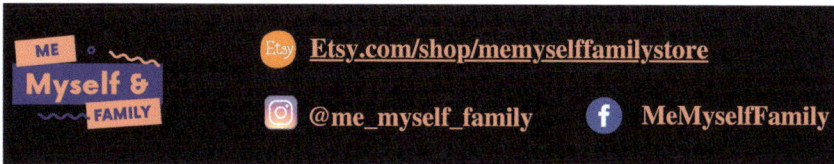

*Affirmation 06.*

## I LIVE A PEACEFUL LIFE.

## 06.     I live a peaceful life.

When you live a peaceful life, you have a balanced feeling. When things get tough, you can handle and understand the bigger picture without being discouraged. Nothing can disturb your inner peace.

When you find peace, you start to identify ways to slow down and enjoy more aspects of your life.

Do less each day. This doesn't mean that you abandon your tasks or appointments- it means that you become more efficient with them.

**_Reflection:_** Examine your commitments and decide what is important. Do you need to multi-task all of the time? Are you leaving time between tasks or appointments?

*Affirmation 07.*

---

**I CREATE AND MAINTAIN HEALTHY BOUNDARIES.**

---

## 07.   I create and maintain healthy boundaries.

When you create healthy boundaries, you are able to control who comes into your life.

Creating healthy boundaries also removes toxic people, habits, behaviors and emotions.

Boundaries should occasionally be revisited so that you can refine them based on life situations.

**_Reflection:_** *Make a list of your current boundaries. Why is each important to you? How do they support your emotional well-being? Are there any boundaries that you need to add to your life? Start small if you have to.*

*Affirmation 08.*

---

**I LEARN SOMETHING NEW EVERYDAY.**

---

## 08.   I learn something new everyday.

When you challenge yourself to learn something new, you gain more knowledge and stimulate your central nervous system.

Learning something new enhances your quality of life and confidence. You become more comfortable with a new topic. Knowledge is power!

It also allows you to enjoy new social groups.

**Reflection:** *What are you curious about? What interests you? Think about things that enhance your quality of life. Talk to people, ask questions, and do your research to learn something new daily.*

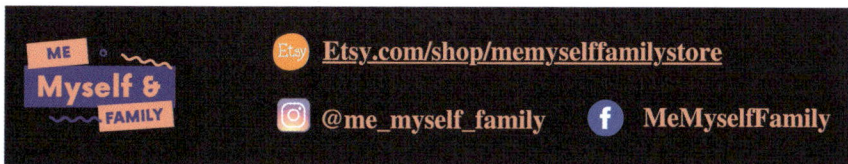

*Affirmation 09.*

**I ENJOY AND APPRECIATE NATURE.**

## 09.     I enjoy and appreciate nature.

Nature is a source for our living conditions. We use natural light, water, and air everyday. Your food and shelter are also provided by nature.

Nature also provides a sense of calmness and peace. The best meditation happens when you're surrounded by the things that provide you with life.

Research shows that taking the time to notice "everyday nature" can boost mental health and well-being.

**_Reflection:_** *How often do you go on walks or hikes, and enjoy the trees and sunlight? Do you encourage your family to plant their own flowers or gardens? Consider these as ways to start appreciating nature. Be mindful and truly appreciate the things that nature can offer to your routine.*

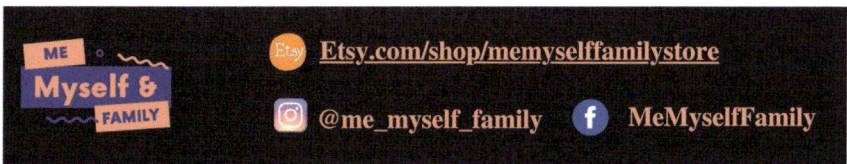

*Affirmation 10.*

**I SHARE MY EXPERIENCES, TO HELP OTHERS.**

## 10. I share my experiences, to help others.

When you share your experiences, you inspire others to keep going. Your experience may be ordinary to you, but it might seem extraordinary to someone else.

Sharing your story also allows you to celebrate your wins and your ability to move forward, which should not go unnoticed.

While sharing your story, you find similarities with other people, which can help you make new friends.

**_Reflection:_** *How transparent are you about your successes or failures? Can you share any wins or lessons learned that would encourage others? Are you proud of what you have accomplished? Share all things safely and understand the impact of your stories.*

*Affirmation 11.*

**I HAVE THE POWER
TO CRUSH MY GOALS.**

## 11. I have the power to crush my goals.

Set yourself up for success by making sure that your goals are **SMART** goals. Your goals should be:

**S**pecific- Be clear and well defined
**M**easurable- Set milestones and measure your success
**A**ttainable- Be realistic. The goal should be achievable
**R**elevant- It moves you in the right direction
**T**ime-bound- Set a deadline for achieving the goal

**Reflection:** *What goals are you still working to achieve? Are they SMART goals? Spend some time reviewing your goals to make sure that they meet the SMART format.*

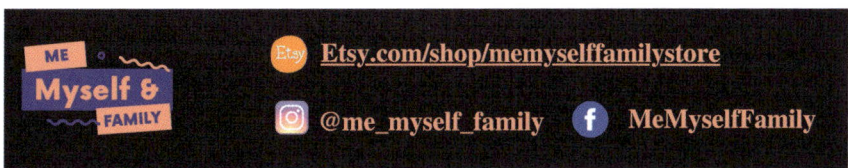

*Affirmation 12.*

**I RELEASE NEGATIVE ENERGY FROM MY LIFE.**

## 12. I release negative energy from my life.

When you release negative energy, you see immediate benefits to your mental health and emotional well-being.

Releasing negative energy removes toxins from the body, while allowing space for physical well being, positivity and hope.

You can think clearly, see red flags, and create healthy boundaries.

**_Reflection:_** *What people, habits, or behaviors bring negative energy to your life? Work to release them, even if it takes time. Be still. Meditate. Find healthy distractions.*

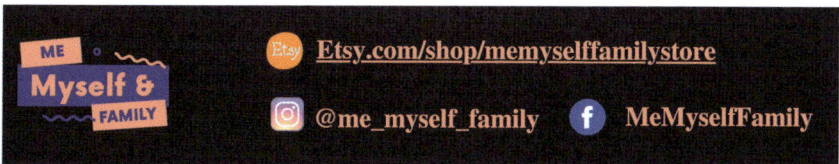

*Affirmation 13.*

---

**MY SMILE BRIGHTENS EVERY SPACE THAT I AM IN.**

---

# 13. My smile brightens every space that I am in.

When you smile, the movement of your facial muscles release naturally-occurring, feel-good chemicals and endorphins.

The endorphins trigger positive feelings and can lower stress levels and improve your mood.

Your smile shows confidence and brings positive energy to any room that you step in.

**_Reflection:_** *Do you make a conscious effort to be present in any space that you are in? How do you shine your light on those around you? Are you easy to be around?*

*Affirmation 14.*

## I USE WISDOM TO MAKE THE BEST DECISIONS.

## 14. I use wisdom to make the best decisions.

A good decision maker chooses outcomes that are the best for themselves and others. It's also an act of compassion and consideration.

When you use wisdom to make good decisions, you are honoring your experiences and any lessons learned during your journey.

Making good decisions also means that you involve others when needed for more knowledge or opinions.

**_Reflection:_** *What is your decision-making process? Do you take your time? Are you able to make quick decisions if needed? How can you stay more open-minded when approached with tough situations?*

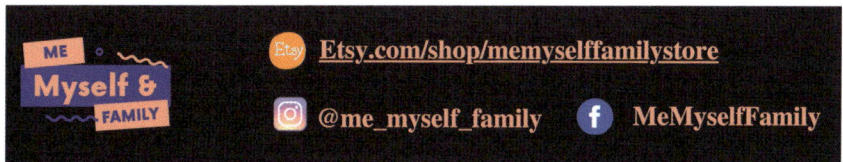

*Affirmation 15.*

**I AM HONEST WITH MYSELF AND OTHERS.**

# 15. I am honest with myself and others.

Being honest with yourself and others is a form of self-care. You are using integrity and mindfulness to make decisions.

Honesty allows you to be clear about who you are, what you want, and who you want to become.

It also allows people to trust your behaviors, actions, motives, and intentions.

**_Reflection:_** *How has honesty paid off for you? Do you like how you present yourself to the world? What are your intentions for yourself and other people?*

## Conclusion

I hope the affirmations provided positivity, hope, and new insight. Let the affirmations guide you into a more peaceful, powerful, and confident life. Revisit them often. Practice them. Meditate on them. Journal your thoughts. For ultimate impact, practice one affirmations each week.

Thank you for your purchase. And for more content, check out my eCourse titled Positive Affirmations That Will Change Your Life. Not only does this 30- minute course give you affirmations for your daily life, but it also provides worksheets to help you on your journey. Whether you listen from your car or at home, be ready to feel inspired.

And for other cool affirmation items like journals and calendars, check out the Me Myself & Family store, and social media accounts:

Instagram- @me_myself_family
Facebook- Me Myself & Family

And don't forget to leave a review!

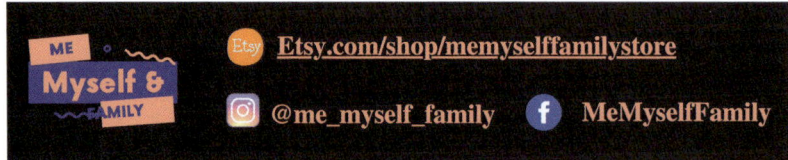

Printed in Great Britain
by Amazon